Edith Nesbit

Royal Children of English History

Nesbit, Edith

Royal Children of English History

ISBN/EAN: 978-3-86741-492-0
First published in 2010 by Europaeischer Hochschulverlag GmbH & Co KG, Bremen, Germany.

© Europaeischer Hochschulverlag GmbH & Co KG, Fahrenheitstr. 1, D-28359 Bremen (www.ehv-online.com). All rights reserved.

This book is a reproduction of an out of print title and has originally been published in 1897. Because no electronic master copies of this title could be obtained, the publisher had to reuse old copies of the text. We therefore apologize for any possible loss in quality.

Edith Nesbit

Royal Children of English History

ALFRED THE GREAT LEARNING TO READ.

CONTENTS

Alfred the Great	1
Prince Arthur	11
Henry the Third	22
The First Prince of Wales	31
Edward the Black Prince	43
Henry the Fifth and the Baby King	54

Royal Children of English History

Alfred the Great.

WHEN I was very, very little, I hated history more than all my other lessons put together, because I had to learn it out of a horrid little book, called somebody's "Outlines of English History"; and it seemed to be all the names of the kings and the dates of battles, and, believing it to be nothing else, I hated it accordingly.

I hope you do not think anything so foolish, because, really, history is a story, a story of things that happened to real live people in our England years ago; and the things that are happening here and now, and that are put in the newspapers, will be history for little children one of these days.

The people in those old times were the same kind of people who live now. Mothers loved their children then, and fathers worked for them, just as mothers and fathers do now, and children then were good or bad, as the case might be, just as little children are now. And the people you read about in history were real live people, who were good and bad, and glad and sorry, just as people are now-a-days.

A.D. 827.

You know that if you were to set out on a journey from one end of England to another, wherever you went, through fields and woods and lanes, you would still be in the kingdom of Queen Victoria. But once upon a time, hundreds of years ago, if a child had set out to ride, he might have begun his ride in the morning in one kingdom, and finished it in the evening in another, because England was not one great kingdom then as it is now, but was divided up into seven pieces, with a king to look after each, and these seven kings were always quarrelling with each other and trying to take each other's kingdom away, just as you might see seven naughty children, each with a plot of garden, trying to take each other's gardens and spoiling each other's flowers in their wicked quarrels. But presently came one King, named Egbert, who was stronger than all the others; so he managed to put himself at the head of all the kingdoms, and he was the first King of *all* England. But though he had got the other kings to give in to him, he did not have at all a peaceful time. There were some very fierce wild pirates, called Danes, who used to come sailing across the North Sea in ships with carved swans' heads at the prow, and hundreds of fighting men aboard. Their own country was bleak and desolate, and they were greedy and wanted the pleasant English land. So they used to come and land in all sorts of places along the seashore, and then they would march across the fields and kill the peaceful farmers, and set fire to their houses, and take their sheep and cows. Or sometimes they would drive them out, and live in the farmhouses themselves. Of course, the English people were not going to stand this; so they were always fighting to drive the Danes away when they came here.

A.D. 871.

Egbert's son allowed the Danes to grow very strong in England, and when he died he left several sons, like the kings in the fairy tales; and the first of these princes was made King, but he could not beat the Danes, and then the second one was made King, but he could not beat the Danes. In the fairy tales, you know, it is always the youngest prince who has all the good fortune, and in this story the same thing happened. This prince did what none of his brothers could do. He drove out the Danes from England, and gave his people a chance of being quiet and happy and good. His name was Alfred.

Like most great men, this King Alfred had a good mother. She used to read to him, when he was little, out of a great book with gold and precious stones on the cover, and inside beautiful songs and poetry. And one day she said to the young princes, who were all very fond of being read to out of this splendid book –

"Since you like the book so much, I will give it to the one who is first able to read it, and to say all the poetry in it by heart."

The eldest prince tried to learn it, but I suppose he did not try hard enough; and the other princes tried, but I fear they were too lazy. But you may be quite sure the youngest prince did the right thing. He learnt to read, and then he set to work to learn the poems by heart; and it was a proud day for him and for the Queen when he was able to say all the beautiful poetry to her. She put the book into his hands for his very own, and they kissed each other with tears of pride and pleasure.

You must not suppose that King Alfred drove out the Danes without much trouble, much thought, and much hard work. Trouble, thought, and hard work are the only three spells the fairies have left us, so of course he had to use them. He was made King just after the Danes had gained a great victory, and for the first eight years of his reign he was fighting them continually. At one time they had conquered almost the whole of England, and they would have killed Alfred if they could have found him.

You know, a wise prince always disguises himself when danger becomes very great. So Alfred disguised himself as a farm labourer, and went to live with a farmer, who used to make him feed the beasts and help about the farm, and had no idea that this labourer was the great King himself.

One day the farmer's wife went out – perhaps she went out to milk the cows; at any rate it was some important business – and she had made some cakes for supper, and she saw Alfred sitting idle in the kitchen, so she asked him to look after the cakes, to see that they did not burn. Alfred said he would. But he had just received some news about the Danes, and he was thinking and thinking and thinking over this, and he forgot all about the cakes, and when the farmer's wife came in she found them burnt black as coal.

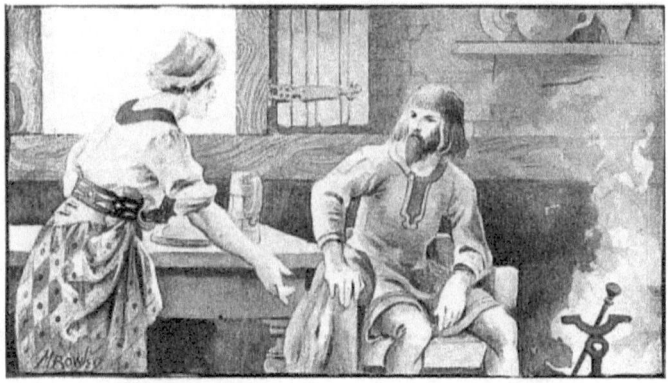

"Oh, you silly, greedy fellow," she said, "you can eat cakes fast enough; but you can't even take the trouble to bake them when other people take the trouble to make them for you."

And I have heard that she even slapped his face. He bore it all very patiently.

"I am very sorry," he said, "but I was thinking of other things."

Just at that moment her husband came in followed by several strangers, and, to the good woman's astonishment, they all fell on their knees and greeted her husband's labourer as their King.

"We have beaten the Danes," they said, "and everyone is asking where is King Alfred? You must come back with us."

"Forgive me," cried the woman. "I didn't think of your being the King."

"Forgive me," said Alfred, kindly. "I didn't think of your cakes being burnt."

"THERE WERE NO CLOCKS IN THOSE DAYS, BUT HE MADE A CLOCK OUT OF A CANDLE."

The Danes had many more fighting men than Alfred; so he was obliged to be very cautious and wise, or he could never have beaten them at all. In those days very few people could read; and the evenings used to seem very long sometimes, so that anybody who could tell a story or sing a song was made much of, and some people made it their trade to go about singing songs and telling stories and making jokes to amuse people who could not sing songs or tell stories or make jokes themselves. These were called gleemen, and wherever they went they were always welcomed and put at a good place at table, and treated with respect and kindness; and in time of war no one ever killed a gleeman, so they could always feel quite safe whatever was going on.

Now Alfred once wanted to know how many Danes there were in a certain Danish camp, and whether they were too strong for him to beat. So he disguised himself as a gleeman and took a harp, for his mother had taught him to sing and play very prettily, and he went and sang songs to the Danes and told stories to them. But all the time he kept his eyes open, and found out all he wanted to know. And he saw that the Danes were not expecting to be attacked by the English people, so that, instead of keeping watch, they were feasting and drinking and playing all their time. Then he went back to his own soldiers, and they crept up to the Danish camp and fell upon it while the Danes were feasting and making merry, and as the Danes were not expecting a fight, the English were easily able to get much the best of it.

At last, after many fights, King Alfred managed to make peace with the Danes, and then he settled down to see what he could do for his own people. He saw that if he was to keep out the wicked Danes he must be able to fight them by sea as well as by land. So he learned how to build ships and taught his people how to build them, and that was the beginning of the great English navy, which you ought to be proud of if you are big enough to read this book. Alfred was wise enough to see that knowledge is power, and, as he wanted his people to be strong, he tried to make them learned. He built schools, and at University College, Oxford, there are people that will tell you that that college was founded by Alfred the Great.

He used to divide up his time very carefully, giving part to study and part to settling disputes among his people, and part to his shipbuilding and his other duties. They had no clocks and watches in those days, and he used sometimes to get so interested in his work as to forget that it was time to leave it and go on to something else, just as you do sometimes when you get so interested in a game of rounders that you forget that it is time to go on with your lessons. The idea of a clock never entered into Alfred's head, at least not a clock with wheels, and hands on its face, but he was so clever that he made a clock out of a candle. He painted rings of different colours round the candle, and when the candle had burnt down to the first ring it was half an hour gone, and when it was burnt to the next ring it was another half-hour, and so on. So he could tell exactly how the time went.

He was called Alfred the Great, and no king has better deserved such a title.

"So long as I have lived," he said, "I have striven

to live worthily." And he longed, above all things, to leave "to the men that came after a remembrance of him in good works."

He did many good and wise things, but the best and wisest thing he ever did was to begin to write the History of England. There had been English poems before this, but no English stories that were not written in poetry. So that Alfred's book was the first of all the thousands and thousands of English books that you see on the shelves of the big libraries. His book is generally called the Saxon Chronicle, and was added to by other people after his death.

He made a number of wise laws. It is believed that it was he who first ordained that an Englishman should be tried not only by a judge but also by a jury of people like himself.

KING ALFRED DISGUISED HIMSELF AS A CLEESMAN & TOOK A HARP & SANG SONGS TO THE DANES & TOLD STORIES TO THEM

A.D. 901.

Though he had fought bravely when fighting was needed to defend his kingdom, yet he loved peace and all the arts of peace. He loved justice and kindness, and little children; and all folk loved and wept for him when he died, because he was a good King who had always striven to live worthily, that is to say, he had always tried to be good.

His last words to his son, just before he died, were these – "It is just that the English people should be as free as their own thoughts."

You must not think that this means that the English people should be free to think as they like or to do as they like. What it means is, that an Englishman should be as free to do good deeds as he is to think good thoughts.

Prince Arthur

A.D. 1066.

THE Danes never succeeded in conquering England and in making it their own, though many of them settled in England and married English wives. But some relations of the Danes, called the Normans, were bolder and stronger and more fortunate. And William, who was called the Conqueror, became King of England, and left his son to rule after him. And when four Norman Kings had reigned in England, the Count of Anjou was made the English King, because his mother was the heiress of the English crown.

His great-grandfather, Ingeger, the first Count of Anjou, must have been a very brave man. When he was quite a boy he was page to his godmother, who was a great lady. It was the custom then for boys of noble family to serve noble ladies as pages.

One morning this lady's husband was found dead in his bed, and the poor lady was accused by a nobleman, named Gontran, of murdering him. Gontran said he was quite sure of her guilt, and that he was ready to stake his life on it, that is to say, he offered to fight anyone who should say that the lady was innocent. This seems a curious way of finding out a person's innocence or guilt, but it was the custom of the times.

The poor lady could find no one who believed in her enough to risk his life, and she began to despair, when suddenly her boy-page rushed forward and begged that, though he was not yet a knight, and so had really no right to fight, yet that he might be allowed to do combat in her defence. "The whole Court were spectators. The Duke Charles was on his throne, and the accused widow in a litter curtained with black. Prayers were offered that God would aid the right. The trumpets sounded, and the champions rode in full career against each other. At the first onset Gontran's lance pierced his adversary's shield so that he could not disengage it, and Ingeger was thus enabled to close with him, hurl him to the ground, and despatch him with a dagger. Then, while the lists rang with applause, the brave boy rushed up to his godmother and threw himself into her arms in a transport of joy."

When William conquered England he became King of England and still owned his own possessions in Normandy, and the Count of Anjou, when he became King, still held the lands he had held as Count, so that the Kings of England held a great part of France as well as England. The Counts of Anjou used to wear a sprig of broom, or *planta genista*, in their helmets, and from this they were called the Plantagenet Kings.

The first of them was brave and clever, and the second was brave, but the third, John, was mean and cruel and cowardly, and had really no right to the throne at all. His nephew, Prince Arthur of Brittany, ought to have been King, because he was the son of John's elder brother. But John wanted the kingdom for himself, and though the King of France tried to help Arthur to get his rights, John would not give up the crown he had stolen. He managed to take Prince Arthur prisoner, and then pretended to be very fond of him. "All this quarrel has been a mistake," he said; "come with me and I will give you a kingdom."

So Prince Arthur went with him, and in the dark night, as they passed along by the river, the wicked King stabbed the young Prince with his own hand, and pushed him into the swift-flowing water. "There," he cried, "that is the kingdom I promised you."

And the poor young Prince sank into the dark flood, never to rise again.

Shakespeare tells another story of Prince Arthur's death, which you will read for yourselves one day; and this is the story: –

After King John had taken the young Prince prisoner, he shut him up in the Castle of Northampton, and ordered Hubert de Burgh, the Governor of the Castle, to put poor Arthur's eyes out, because he thought that no one would want a blind boy to be King of England. So Hubert went into the room where the little Prince was shut up.

"Good morning," said the Prince. "You are sad, Hubert."

"Indeed, I have been merrier," said Hubert, who, though he did not like to disobey the King, was yet miserable at the wicked deed he had been asked to do.

"Nobody," said Arthur, "should be sad but I. If I were out of prison and kept sheep I should be as merry as the day is long. And so I would be here but for my uncle. He is afraid of me and I of him. Is it my fault that I was Geoffrey's son? Indeed it is not, and I would to heaven I were your son, so you would love me, Hubert."

"If I talk to him," said Hubert to himself, "I shall never have the courage to do this wicked deed."

"Are you ill, Hubert?" Arthur went on. "You look pale to-day. If you were ill I would sit all night and watch you, for I believe I love you more than you do me."

Hubert dared not listen. He felt he must do the King's wicked will, so he pulled out the paper on which the King had written his cruel order, and showed it to the young Prince. Arthur read it calmly and then turned to Hubert.

"So you are to put out my eyes with hot irons?"

"Young boy, I must," said Hubert.

"And you will?" asked Arthur.

And Hubert answered, "And I will."

"Have you the heart?" cried Arthur. "Do you remember when your head ached how I tied it up with my own handkerchief, and sat up with you the whole night holding your hand and doing everything I could for you! Many a poor man's son would have lain still and never have spoke a loving word to you; but you, at your sick service, had a prince. Will you put out my eyes – those eyes that never did, nor never shall, so much as frown on you?"

"I have sworn to do it," said Hubert. He called two men, who brought in the fire and the hot irons, and the cord to bind the little Prince.

"Give me the irons," said Hubert, "and bind him

here."

"For heaven's sake, Hubert, let me not be bound," cried Arthur. "I will not struggle – I will stand stone still. Nay, hear me, Hubert, drive these men away and I will sit as quiet as a lamb, and I will forgive you whatever torment you may put me to."

And Hubert was moved by his pleading, and told the men to go; and as they went they said – "We are glad to have no part in such a wicked deed as this."

Then Arthur flung his arms round Hubert and implored him to spare his eyes, and at last Hubert consented, for all the time his heart had been sick at the cruel deed he had promised to do. Then he took Prince Arthur away and hid him, and told the King he was dead.

But King John's lords were so angry when they heard that Arthur was dead, and John seemed so sorry for having given the order to Hubert, that Hubert thought it best to tell him that Arthur had not been killed at all, but was still alive and safe. John was now so terrified at the anger of his lords on Arthur's account that Arthur might from that time have been safe from him. But the poor boy was so frightened by what he had gone through that he made up his mind to risk his life in trying to escape. So he decided to leap down from the top of the tower as his only means of escape.

Then he thought he could get away in disguise without being recognised.

"The wall is high, and yet will I leap down," he said. "Good ground, be pitiful and hurt me not."

So he leaped, but the tower was high, and the fall killed him. And before he died, he murmured – "Heaven take my soul and England keep my bones."

That is the story as Shakespeare gives it.

Almost everyone in England hated King John, even before this dreadful affair of Prince Arthur's death. The King of France took Normandy away from him, and his own people would not help him to fight for it.

He was very cruel and revengeful, and often put people in prison or killed them without giving any reason for it, or having them properly tried. So the great nobles of England joined together and said that they would not let John be King any longer in England unless he would give them a written promise to behave better in future. At first he laughed at the idea, and said he should do as he chose, and that he would fight the lords and keep them in their proper place. But he had to give in when he found that only seven of the lords of England were on his side and all the rest against him. So then he asked the barons and the bishops to meet him at Runnymede and there he put his big seal to a writing, promising what they wished. He did not sign his name to it, but you can see that very parchment sealed in the British Museum with the King's big seal to it.

Magna Charta
A.D. 1215.

But though he fixed his seal to the paper he did not keep the promises that were in it, and the barons grew so angry that they asked the King of France to help them to fight John, and to turn him out.

John ran away when he heard that the French were coming. He left his friends to fight his battles, and went off, wrecking the castles of the barons who had asked the French Prince to come over, and who were now with him. Then someone told the barons that the French Prince was determined to cut off all their heads as soon as he had got England for his own. So they saw how foolish they had been to ask him to come and help them. John was in Lincolnshire, and was coming across the sands at the Wash, but the tide suddenly came in and swept away his crown, his treasure, his food, and everything was lost in the sea. King John was very miserable at losing all his treasures, and he tried to drown his sorrows by drinking a lot of beer and eating much more than was good for him. This brought on a fever, and he died miserably, with no one at all to be sorry for him.

A.D. 1216.

He was and is the best-hated of all our English kings.

There was much danger in travelling in those days, for robbers used to hide in the woods and lonely places, and to attack and rob travellers. Many of the nobles themselves who were in attendance on the King, being often unable to get their proper pay, either belonged to these robber bands or secretly helped them, and shared with them the plunder they took from those they robbed. The best known of these robbers was the famous Robin Hood, who lived in the time of King Richard and King John. He is supposed to have been a nobleman, and to have had his hiding place in Sherwood Forest, and he is said to have been kind and merciful to the poor, and to have helped them out of the money and good things he stole from the rich. Many songs about him have come down to us. The poor suffered in those old days many and great hardships at the hands of the nobles of England, who indeed robbed and oppressed them very cruelly. So they were ready enough to sing the praises of one who stole only from the rich and who gave to the poor.

Henry the Third.

A.D. 1216.

HENRY THE THIRD was crowned at Gloucester when he was only nine years old. You remember that King John's crown had been lost in the Wash with his other treasures, so they crowned Henry with a gold bracelet of his mother's. The lords who attended the coronation banquet wore white ribbons round their heads as a sign of their homage to the innocent, helpless child. They made him swear to do as his father had promised in the great charter sealed at Runnymede; and the Earl of Pembroke was appointed to govern the kingdom till Henry grew up.

Henry grew up unlike his cruel father. He was gentle, tenderhearted, fond of romance, music and poetry, sculpture, painting and architecture. Some of the most beautiful churches we have were built in his reign. But, though he had so many good qualities, he had no bravery, no energy and perseverance. He was fond of pleasure and of the beautiful things of this world, and cared too little for the beautiful things of the soul. He was fond of gaiety, and his young queen was of the same disposition. She was one of four sisters. Two of these sisters married kings and two married counts, and the kings' wives were so proud of being queens that they used to make their sisters, the countesses, sit on little low stools while they themselves sat on handsome high chairs.

Henry's time passed in feasts and songs and dancing. Romances and curious old Breton ballads were translated into English, and recited at the Court with all sorts of tales of love and battle and chivalry.

The object of chivalry was to encourage men in noble and manly exercises, and to teach them to succour the oppressed, to uphold the dignity of women, and to help the Christian faith. And chivalry was made attractive by all sorts of gay and pretty devices. Knights used to wear in their helmets a ribbon or a glove that some lady had given them, and it was supposed that, while they had the precious gift of a good lady in their possession, they would do nothing base or disloyal that should dishonour the gift they carried.

Each young noble at twelve years old was placed as page in some other noble household. There, for two years, he learned riding and fencing, and the use of arms. When the lord killed a deer the pages skinned it and carried it home. At a feast the pages carried in the chief dishes and poured the wine for their lords to drink. They helped the ladies of the house in many ways, and carried their trains on state occasions.

At fourteen a page became a squire. He helped his lord to put on his armour, carried his shield to battle, cleaned and polished his lord's armour and sharpened his sword, and he was allowed to wear silver spurs instead of iron ones, such as the common people wore.

When he was considered worthy to become a knight he went through a ceremony which dedicated him to the service of God.

The day before he was to become a knight the young man stripped and bathed. Then he put on a white tunic – the white as a promise of purity; a red robe – the red meant the blood he was to shed in fighting for the right; and he put on a black doublet (which is a sort of jacket), and this was black in token of death, of which a knight was never to be afraid. Then he went into the church, and there he spent the night in prayer. He heard the priests singing their chant in the darkness of the big church, and he thought of his sins, and steadfastly purposed to lead a new life. In the morning he confessed his sins, walked up to the altar, laid down his belt and sword, and then knelt at the foot of the altar steps. He received the Holy Communion, and then the lord who was to make him a knight gave him the accolade – three strokes on the back of the bare neck with the flat side of the sword – and said:

"In the name of Saint George I make thee a knight," – and bade him take back his sword – "in the name of God and Saint George, and use it like a true knight as a terror and punishment for evil-doers, and a defence for widows and orphans, and the poor, and the oppressed, and the priests – the servants of God."

The priests and the ladies came round him and put on his gilt spurs, and his coat of mail, and his breastplate, and armpieces, and gauntlets, and took the sword and girded it on him. Then the young man swore to be faithful to God, the King, and woman; his squire brought him his helmet, and his horse's shoes rang on the church pavement and under the tall arches as his squire led the charger up the aisle. In the presence of priests, and knights, and ladies assembled, the young knight sprang upon his horse and caracoled before the altar, brandishing his lance and his sword. And then away to do the good work he was sworn to.

Many, of course, forgot their promises and broke their vows, but in those wild times many a rough man was made gentle, many a cruel man less cruel, and many a faint-hearted one made bold by the noble thoughts from which the idea of chivalry sprang.

Now, you know, England is governed by the Queen and Parliament. But in those old days England was ruled by the King and by such nobles as had money and strength enough to be able to rule by force. These nobles were indeed a terror to the people. They lived in strong, stoutly-built castles, with a great moat or ditch round them, and having always many retainers and armed servants, they were often able to resist the King himself. It was the growing power and riches of the King which they most dreaded, for he only could do them harm. It was then for their own sakes – to guard their own persons, to protect their own property against the King – rather than from any desire to help the people, that the barons resisted first John and then Henry.

But among them was a noble, unselfish man, who loved his fellow countrymen, and who saw, that to make people rich, and happy, and prosperous, they must be allowed to share in the government of the country in which they live. This noble Englishman, Simon de Montfort, was called the great Earl, and it was he who headed the resistance to Henry the Third, when that King tried to escape from keeping the promises contained in the Great Charter which he had bound himself to obey.

The resistance grew so strong that at last there was war in England. At the Battle of Lewes, Simon de Montfort defeated Henry and took him prisoner, and with him was his son, Prince Edward. Then at last a Parliament was called. Two knights were sent to it from each county, and from every town two citizens. It was chiefly to get these towns represented in Parliament that the great Earl opposed the King.

Prince Edward was very anxious to escape and fight another battle for his father. So he pretended to be very ill. When he got better he asked his gaolers to let him go out riding for the benefit of his health. They agreed, but of course, they sent a guard of soldiers out with him to see that he did not escape. Prince Edward rode out for several days with them and never even tried to get away. But one day he begged them to ride races with each other, while he looked on. They did so, and when their horses were quite tired, he shouted, "I have long enough enjoyed the pleasure of your company, gentlemen, and I bid you good-day," put spurs to his horse, and was soon out of their reach. His friend, the Earl of Gloucester, joined him, and they soon raised an army and defeated the great Earl at Evesham.

A.D. 1265.

"Let us commend our souls to God," said Simon, as Prince Edward and his men came down upon him and the little band of knights who stood by his side. One by one the knights fell, till Simon only was left. He hacked his way through his foes, and had nearly escaped when his horse was brought to the ground, and a death wound was given him from behind. "It is God's grace," he said, and died. But though the leader died, the work was done, and a Parliament established in England.

Some of the priests in England had grown very wicked and greedy. They neglected their duties and thought only of feasting and making themselves comfortable. But some good monks came over from Rome, and determined to try to show the English priests what a Christian's duty was. They made a vow to be poor, and to deny themselves everything, except just enough food to keep body and soul together. They would not even have books at first, but spent all the money they could collect on the poor. They nursed the sick and helped the unfortunate. They would not wear pretty clothes or beautiful vestments, but were dressed in plain grey or black serge, with a rope round the waist, and bare feet. Although they were foreigners and could speak but little English, they encouraged people to write in the English language instead of in Latin or French.

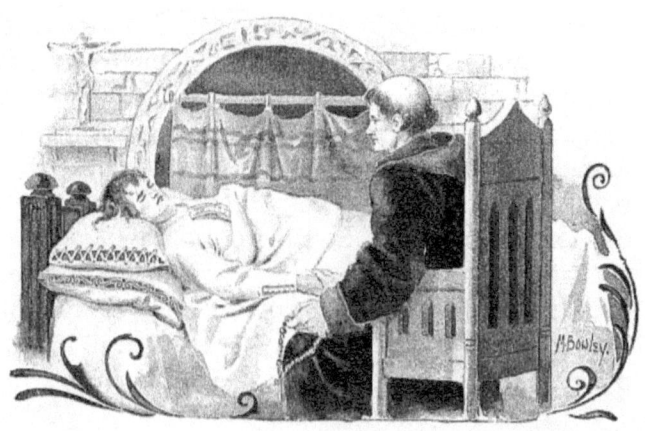

It was a favourite dream of the early English and French kings to take Jerusalem and the Holy Land from the hands of the Saracens, and to let Christians be the guardians of the place where Christ lived and died. To do this they were constantly making war on the Saracens, and these wars were called Crusades, and the knights who went to them Crusaders. Crusaders carried a red cross on their banners and on their shields. The Saracens' banners and shields had a crescent like a new moon. For two hundred years this fighting went on, and the last of our English princes to take part in it was Prince Edward. He had only three hundred knights with him, and was not able to attack Jerusalem, because he could not get together more than seven thousand men. His knights went on pilgrimage to Jerusalem, but he stayed in his camp at Acre. One day a messenger came into his tent with letters, and while he was reading them the wicked messenger stabbed him. He had been sent to do so by the Saracens, because they were afraid of this brave prince. The prince caught the blow on his arm, and kicked the messenger to the ground, but the man rose and rushed at him again with the knife. The dagger just grazed the prince's forehead, and seizing a wooden footstool Prince Edward dashed out the messenger's brains. His wife, the Princess Eleanor, was afraid the dagger was poisoned. So she sucked the blood from his wound with her own lips, and so most likely saved his life. But he was very ill in spite of this, and England nearly lost one of her best and bravest princes.

A.D. 1272.

As soon as he was well enough to travel, he set out for England, and on the way he was met with the sad news that his father and two of his children were dead. So he became King of England, and he was the father of the first Prince of Wales.

The First Prince of Wales

THERE were Welsh princes long before there were English kings, and the Welsh princes could not bear to be subject to the kings of England. So they were always fighting to get back their independence. But the English kings could not let them be free as they wished, because England could never have been safe with an independent kingdom so close to her. So there were constant wars between the two countries, and sometimes the fortune of battle went one way and sometimes the other.

But at last the Welsh Prince Llewellyn was killed. He had gone to the south of Wales to cheer up his subjects there, and he had crossed the river Wye into England, when a small band of English knights came up. A young knight named Adam Frankton met with a Welsh chief as he came out of a barn to join the Welsh army. Frankton at once attacked him, and after a struggle, wounded the Welsh chief to death. Then he rode on to battle, and when he came back he tried to find out what had become of the Welshman. He heard that he was already dead, and then they found that the dead man was the great Welsh Prince Llewellyn. His head was taken off and sent to London, where it was placed on the battlements of the Tower and crowned, in scorn, with ivy. This was because an old Welsh magician, years before, had said that when English money became round, the Welsh princes should be crowned in London. And money had become round in this way: –

Before this there were silver pennies, and when anyone wanted a half-penny, he chopped the silver penny in two, and if he wanted a farthing he chopped the silver penny in four, so that money was all sorts of queer shapes. But Edward the First had caused round copper half-pennies and farthings to be made, and when the Welsh prince had heard of this he had believed that the old magician's words were coming true, and that he should defeat Edward and become king of England himself. Instead of this, the poor man's head was cut off, and, in mockery of his hopes and dreams, they crowned the poor dead head with the wreath of ivy.

Now the Welsh wanted another prince, and King Edward said: "If you will submit to me and not fight any more, you shall have a prince who was born in Wales, can speak never a word of English, and never did wrong to man, woman, or child." The Welsh people agreed that if they could have such a prince as that, they would be contented and quiet, and give up fighting. And so one day the leaders of the Welsh met King Edward at his castle in Caernarvon and asked for the Prince he had promised them, and he came out of his castle with his little son, who had only been born a week before, in his arms.

"Here is your Prince," he said, holding up the little baby. "He was born in Wales, he cannot speak a word of English, and he has never done harm to man, woman or child."

Instead of being angry at the trick the king had played them, the Welsh people were very pleased. Welsh nurses took care of the baby, so that he really did learn to speak in Welsh before he could speak in English. And the Welsh were so pleased with their baby king that from that time Edward the First had no more trouble with them.

There are many stories told of this prince's boldness as a child. He promised them to grow up as brave as his father, and it would have been better for him if he had done so. He was always very fond of hunting, and once when he was quite young, he and his servants were hunting the deer. His servants lost the trace of the deer, and presently, when they reined up their horses, they found that the young prince was no longer with them. They looked everywhere for him, very frightened lest he should have fallen into the hands of robbers; and at last they heard a horn blown in the forest. They followed the sound of it and presently found that the young prince had seen which way the deer went, and had followed it and killed it all by himself.

Now King Edward the First had great trouble with his Scotch nobles, and many were the battles he fought with them, until at last he forced the Scottish king Balliol to declare himself his vassal, and he became the over-lord of Scotland. But there arose a brave Scot named William Wallace, who longed to see his country free from England, and he drove the English back, and again and again he beat them.

But in a few years Edward got together another army, and leading them into Scotland he beat the Scots and took Wallace prisoner. Wallace was tried and found guilty of treason, and when he had been beheaded, they crowned his head with laurel and placed it on London Bridge, for all the passers-by, by road or river, to see.

A.D. 1305.

Then two men claimed the Scottish crown, Robert Bruce and John, who was called the Red Comyn. They were jealous of each other, and Bruce thought that Comyn had betrayed him. They met in a church to have an explanation.

"You are a traitor," said Bruce.

"You lie," said Comyn.

And Bruce in a fury struck at him with his dagger, and then, filled with horror, rushed from the church. "To horse, to horse," he cried. One of his attendants, named Kirkpatrick, asked him what was the matter.

"I doubt," said Bruce, "that I have slain the Red Comyn."

"You doubt!" said Kirkpatrick. "I will make sure."

So saying, he hurried back into the church and killed the wounded man.

And now the task of defending Scotland against Edward was left to Robert Bruce. King Edward was so angry when he heard of this murder, that at the feast, when his son was made a knight, he swore over the swan, which was the chief dish and which was the emblem of truth and constancy, that he would never rest two nights in the same place till he had chastised the Scots. And for some time the Scots and English were at bitter war, and when King Edward died, he made his son promise to go on fighting.

A.D. 1307.

But Edward the Second was not a man like his father. He was more like his grandfather Henry the Third, caring for pretty colours and pretty things, rich clothes, rich feasts, rich jewels, and surrounding himself with worthless favourites. Robert Bruce said he was more afraid of the dead bones of Edward the First than of the living body of Edward of Caernarvon, and that it was easier to win a kingdom from his son than a foot of land from the father. Gradually the castles the English had taken in Scotland were won back from them. For twenty years the English had held the Castle of Edinburgh, and at the end of that time, Randolph, a Scottish noble, came to besiege it.

The siege was long, and the brave English showed no signs of giving in. Randolph was told that it was possible to climb up the south face of the rock on which the castle stood, and steep as the rock was, Randolph and some others began to climb it one dark night. When they were part of the way up, and close to the wall of the castle, they heard a soldier above them cry out – "Away, I see you," and down came stone after stone. Had many more been thrown Randolph and his companions must have been dashed to the ground and killed, for it was only on a very narrow ledge that they had found a footing. But the soldier was only in joke, trying to frighten his fellows. He had not really seen them at all, and he passed on. When all was quiet again, the daring Scots climbed up till they reached the top of the wall, and when they had fixed a rope ladder the rest of their men came up. Then they fell upon the men of the garrison and killed them, and the castle was taken by the Scots.

A.D. 1314.

But a greater loss awaited the English. Edward led an English army to battle in Scotland; and at Bannockburn they met the force of the Scots king. They fought till the field was slippery with blood, and covered with broken armour and lances and arrows. Then at the last, as the English began to waver, Bruce charged down on them with more soldiers and utterly routed them. Edward with difficulty saved his life, and throughout England there were bitter lamentings at the loss and shame the country had suffered. Scotland was free from the English yoke, and of all the great conquests the first Edward had won, only Berwick-on-Tweed remained to the English.

Edward II. was never loved by his subjects. He made favourites of silly and wicked persons, and so gave much offence to good folk. He was wasteful and extravagant, and did not even try to govern the country wisely and well, while his favourites made themselves hated more and more by their dishonesty and wickedness. The last of his favourites was named Despenser, and he was as much hated by the Queen Isabella as by the lords and people of England. Despenser not only made himself hated by the queen, but he managed also to make her dislike her husband, the king, with whom she had long been on unfriendly terms. At last Isabella, disgusted with her husband and his favourite, ran away to France, and there, with the help of the Count of Hainault and other friends in England, she raised an army and attacked and defeated her husband and his favourite. The young Despenser was hanged on a gibbet fifty feet high, and a Parliament was called to decide what should be done with the king.

The Parliament declared its right to make or unmake kings, and ordered that Edward should not be king any more. Some members went to Edward at Kenilworth to tell him what they had decided, and

Edward clad in a plain black gown, received them and quietly promised to be king no more. Then he was taken to Berkeley Castle, and a few months after the people learned that he was dead.

There has always been much doubt whether he died a natural death or was murdered. The Bishop of Hereford, who had always been on the queen's side, is said to have sent to two wicked men the following message written in Latin – "Edwardum occidere nolite timere bonum est." Now this message had two meanings according to the way the stops were put in. The first was – "Be unwilling to fear to kill Edward – it is good." The other was – "Be unwilling to kill Edward – it is good to fear."

So you see that, if this message fell into anyone's hands for whom it was not intended, the bishop would have been able to say he meant to warn people not to kill the king, while Gurney and Maltravers, who received the message, could say that the paper was an order to kill him. The story goes, that they came to the castle and there found the poor king in a dungeon. He was standing in mire and puddle, and, although he was a king, they gave him only bread and water. Then he thought of his former greatness and how brave and gallant a show he had made as a knight, and he cried out –

> "Tell Isabel, the queen, I looked not thus
> When for her sake I ran at tilt in France
> And there unhorsed the Duke of Cleremont."

A.D. 1327.

He was too weak to resist these wicked men, and they had no mercy in their hearts, but murdered him.

A.D. 1340.

THE name of Edward the Black Prince will always be remembered with love and admiration by all young Englishmen, because he was by all accounts a very brave, gallant, and courteous prince, feared by his foes and by his friends beloved. His father, Edward the Third, had not given up his hopes of regaining his lost possessions in France, so he spent two long years in getting together money and ships and an army. He fought the French fleet near Sluys. Both sides fought fiercely, and at last the English won. The French had thought that they were quite sure to get the best of it, and they were afraid to tell the King of France how the English had beaten them, for hundreds of the French had been either killed or been forced to jump into the sea to escape the swords of the English.

Now, at this time every king kept a jester to make jokes and amuse him and his friends at their feasts, and the jester was a privileged person, who could say anything he liked. So now they told the jester of the King of France that he must tell the king the bad news, because he could say what he liked and no one would punish him for it. So the jester said –

"Oh! what dastardly cowards the English are!"

"How so?" said the king, who expected to hear that the cowardly English had been driven away by his men.

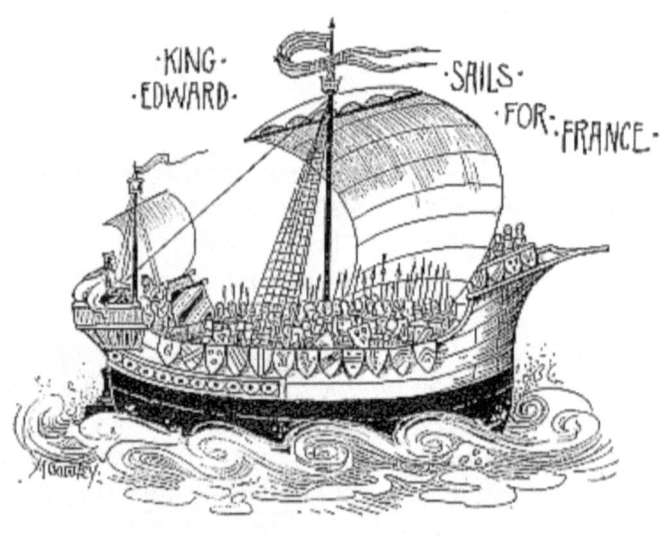

"Because," answered the jester, "they have not jumped into the sea as our brave men had to do."

So then the king asked him what he meant, and then the courtiers came forward and told the sad story of the English victory.

Then Edward besieged a town called Tournay, but he had not enough money to get provisions for his men, so he had to make friends with the king of France for a little while and go back to England.

Six years later he pawned his crown and his queen's jewels, and at last got together enough money to go and fight with the French again. He landed at La Hogue, and as he landed he fell so violently that his nose began to bleed.

"Oh, this is a bad sign," said his courtiers, "that your first step on French soil should be a fall."

"Not so," said the king. "It is a good sign. It shows that the land desires me: so she takes me close to her."

He had thirty-two thousand men with him, and his son, the Black Prince. Some say he was called the Black Prince because he wore black armour, but others say it was because he made himself as great a terror to the French as a black night is to foolish children.

Edward marched towards the French and the French marched to meet him, and as they marched they broke down all the bridges, so that the English could not advance by them. But Edward had made up his mind to get across the river Seine and fight with his enemies; and he was no more to be stopped by the water than a dog would have been who wanted to get over to the other side to fight another dog. He got a poor man to show him a place where the river was shallow at low tide, and there he plunged into the river, crying, "Let him who loves me follow me," and the whole army followed and got safely to the other side.

Edward arranged his soldiers well, and went himself to the top of a little hill where there was a windmill. From this he could see everything that went on. The French had a far larger army than the English, and when they came in sight of Edward's army and saw how well placed it was, the wiser Frenchmen said, "Do not let us fight them to-day, for our men and horses are tired. Let us wait for to-morrow and then we can drive them back." So the foremost of the French army turned back, but those behind were discontented and thought the fighting had begun and that they had not had a chance. So they pushed forward till the whole French army was close to the English.

A.D. 1346.

King Edward had made all his soldiers sit on the grass and eat and drink. Mounted on his horse he rode among them telling them to be brave, for that they were now going to win a glorious victory and cover themselves with eternal glory. At three in the afternoon the first French soldiers came face to face with the Englishmen, and the battle began. Some soldiers from Genoa who had been paid to fight for the French king, said they did not want to fight, they were too tired and could not fight as good soldiers should, but the men behind pressed them on and they were beaten. A heavy rain fell, with thunder, and a great flight of crows hovered in the air over all the battalions, making a loud noise. Shortly afterwards it cleared up and the sun shone very bright. But the French had it in their faces and the English at their backs.

When the Genoese drew near, they approached the English with a loud noise to frighten them; but the English remained quite quiet, and did not seem to attend to it. They then set up a second shout and advanced a little forward. The English never moved. Still they hooted a third time, and advanced with their crossbows presented and began to shoot. The English archers then moved a step forward and shot their arrows with such force and quickness that it seemed as if it snowed. The fight raged furiously, and presently a knight came galloping up to the windmill and begged the king to send help to his son, the Black Prince, as he was sore pressed.

"Is my son in danger of his life?" said the king.

"No, thank God," returned the knight, "but in great need of your help."

Then the king answered: "Return to them that sent you and say that I command them to let the boy win his spurs, for I am determined that, if it please God, all the glory of this day shall be given to him and to those to whose care I have entrusted him."

This message cheered the Prince mightily, and he and the English won the battle of Creçy.

And the battle of Creçy, one of the most glorious in English History, was won by the common people of England, yeomen and archers, foot soldiers against the knights and squires of France with their swords and horses.

In this battle the blind king of Bohemia took part with the French.

"I pray you," he said to his friends, "lead me into the battle that I may strike one more stroke with this good sword of mine."

So they led him in and he was killed.

A.D. 1356.

The battle of Poictiers was fought entirely under the direction of the Black Prince, and this was another splendid victory to England; and in this battle the French king was taken. The king was brought to the Black Prince as he was resting in his tent, and he behaved like the true gentleman he was. He showed the deepest respect and sympathy for his vanquished foe. He ordered the best of suppers to be served to the king, and would not sit with him to eat, but stood behind his chair and waited on him like a servant, saying – "I am only a prince. It is not fitting I should sit in the presence of the king of France." And King John said –

"Since it has pleased Heaven that I am a captive, I thank my God I have fallen into the hands of the most generous and valiant prince alive."

King John was taken as a prisoner to London. They rode into the city, King John mounted on a beautiful white horse that belonged to the Black Prince, while Prince Edward himself, riding on a black pony, was ready to wait on him, and to do his bidding.

It was this generous temper which made the Black Prince beloved by all who knew him; it was only during his last illness that his character seemed to be changed by the great sufferings that he underwent, and it was only during the last year of his life that he did anything of which a king and an Englishman need be ashamed.

He seems to have inherited his skill in war from his father, and from his mother, Queen Philippa, he inherited gentleness, goodness, and true courtesy. There are many stories told of the goodness and courage of this lady. Among others, this: –

A.D. 1347.

When Edward the Third had besieged Calais for a year, the good town which had held out so long was obliged to surrender, for there was no longer anything to eat in the city, and the folks said: "It is as good to die by the hands of the English as to die here by famine like rats in a hole." So they sent to tell the king they would give up the town to him. But Edward the Third was so angry with them for having resisted him so long, that he said that they should all be hanged. Then Edward the Black Prince begged his father not to be so hard on brave men who had only done what they believed to be their duty, and entreated him to spare them. Then said the king –

"I will spare them on condition that six citizens, bare-headed and bare-footed, clad only in their shirts, with ropes round their necks, shall come forth to me here, bringing the keys of the city."

And when the men of Calais heard this, they said: "No; better to die than live a dishonoured life by giving up even one of these our brothers who have fought and suffered with us." But one of the chief gentlemen of Calais – Eustace de S. Pierre – said:

"It is good that six of us should win eternal glory in this world and the sunshine of God's countenance in the next, by dying for our town and our brethren. I, for one, am willing to go to the English king on such terms as he commands."

Then up rose his son and said likewise, and four other gentlemen, inspired by their courage, followed their example. So the six in their shirts, with ropes round their necks and the keys of the town in their hands, went out through the gates, and all the folk of

Calais stood weeping and blessing them as they went. When they came to the king, he called for the hangman, saying – "Hang me these men at once."

But Queen Philippa was there, and though she was ill, she left her tent weeping so tenderly that she could not stand upright. Therefore she cast herself upon her knees before the king, and spoke thus: –

"Ah, gentle sire, from the day I passed over sea I have asked for nothing; now I pray you, for the love of Our Lady's son Christ, to have mercy on these."

King Edward waited for a while before speaking, and looked at the queen as she knelt, and he said – "Lady, I had rather you had been elsewhere. You pray so tenderly that I dare not refuse you; and though I do it against my will, nevertheless take them. I give them to you."

Then took he the six citizens by the halters and delivered them to the queen, and released from death all those of Calais for the love of her.

Henry the Fifth and the Baby King

A.D. 1399.

HENRY the Fourth was the Black Prince's nephew, and he came to be king of England. His son was Henry the Fifth, the greatest of the Plantagenet kings. When he was a young man, and only Prince of Wales, he was very wild and fond of games and jokes. They used to call him Harry Madcap.

Once, when he got into some trouble or other, his father, who was ill, sent for him, and he went at once in a fine dress that he had had made for a fancy dress party. It was of light blue satin with odd puckers in the sleeves, and at every pucker the tailor had left a little bit of blue thread and a tag like a needle. The king was very angry with the prince for daring to come into the royal presence in such a silly coat. Then Prince Harry said –

"Dear father, as soon as I heard that you wanted me, I was in such a hurry to come to you that I had no time to even think of my coat, much less change it."

And so the king forgave him.

Another time one of his servants got into trouble and was taken before the Chief Judge Sir William Gascoyne. The Prince went directly to the Court where the judge was and said –

"Lord Judge, this is my servant, and you must let him go, for I am the king's son."

"No," said the judge, "I sit here in the place of the king himself, to do justice to all his subjects, and were this man the Prince of Wales himself, instead of being his servant, he should be punished in that he has offended against the law."

The prince was so angry that he actually forgot himself so far as to strike Sir William Gascoyne. The good judge did not hesitate a minute.

"You have insulted the king himself," he said, "in my person, since I sit here in his place to do justice. The common folks who offend against the law offend merely against the king; but you, young man, are a double traitor to your king and your father."

And he sent the prince to prison.

Henry begged the good judge's pardon afterwards, and when he came to the throne he thanked him for having behaved so justly and wisely, and gave him great honour because he had not been afraid to do his duty without respect of rank, and Henry behaved to the judge like a good son to a good father.

No king of England was ever more wise or brave or just than Henry the Fifth; and even now he is remembered with affection. One of Shakespeare's most splendid plays is written about him, and, when you have once read that, you will always remember and love Henry the Fifth as all Englishmen should do.

A.D. 1413.

At the very beginning of his reign the wars with France began again. The king sent to France and claimed some lands that had belonged to Edward the Third; and the young prince of France sent back the message – "There is nothing in France that can be won with a dance or a song. You cannot get dukedoms in France by playing and feasting, and the prince sends you something that will suit you better than lands in France. He has sent you a barrel of tennis balls, and bids you play with them and let serious matters be." Then King Henry was very angry, and said – "We thank him for his present.

When we have matched our rackets to these balls,
We will in France, by God's grace, play a set
Shall strike his father's crown into the hazard.

Before I was King of England I was wild and merry because I knew not how great and solemn a state waited for me. I have played in my youth like a common man because I was only Prince of Wales; but now that I am King of England I will rise up with so full of glory that I will dazzle all the eyes of France."

Henry sailed over to France and besieged a town called Harfleur. He spoke to the soldiers before they attacked the town.

"Break down the wall and go through," he said, "or close the wall up with our English dead.

Bend every spirit
To his full height. On, on, you noblest English,
Whose blood is fetched from fathers of war proof.
Be copy now to men of grosser blood
And teach them how to war. And you, good yeomen,
Whose limbs were made in England, let us swear
That you are worth your breeding, which I doubt not;
Cry God for Harry, England and Saint George."

The Englishmen answered nobly to his appeal, and Harfleur was taken.

Then the English advanced to a place called Agincourt, a name fated to be linked with splendid glory for ever in the hearts of all English folk. The French had a very large army, and the English soldiers were tired with their long march. Many of them were ill and many were hungry; but they loved the king, and for his sake, and for the sake of their country, they were brave in spite of hunger and cold. Though they were in a strange country and many times outnumbered by their foes, they kept up a brave heart as Englishmen have done, thank God, many's the good time, all the world over. So few were they that the Earl of Westmoreland said, just before the battle, –

"Oh, that we now had here
But one ten thousand of those men in England
That do no work to-day!"

The king came in just as he was saying this, and said –

"No, if we are marked to die, we are enough for our country to lose. If we are to live, the fewer there are of us the greater share of honour. I do not covet gold or feasting, or fine garments, but honour I do covet. Wish not another man from England. I would not lose the honour of this fight by sharing it with more men than are here, and if any among our soldiers has no desire to fight, let him go. He shall have a passport and money to take him away. I should be ashamed to die in such a man's company. We need not wish for men from England. It is the men in England who will envy us when they hear of the great crown of honour and glory that we have won this day. This is Saint Crispin's day. Every man who fights on this day will remember it and be honoured to the last hour of his life. Crispin's day shall ne'er go by from this day to the ending of the world,

But we in it shall be remembered,
We few, we happy few, we band of brothers,

For he to-day that sheds his blood with me
Shall be my brother, be he ne'er so vile.
And gentlemen in England now abed
Shall think themselves accursed they were not here,
And hold their manhood cheap while any speaks
That fought with us upon St. Crispin's day."

Lord Salisbury came in as the king was saying this. "The French are in battle order," he said, "and ready to charge upon our men."

"All things are ready," said the king quietly, "if our minds are ready."

"Perish the man whose mind is backward now," said Westmoreland.

"You wish no more for men from England then," said the king smiling.

And Westmoreland, inspired with courage and confidence by the king's brave speech, answered – "I would to God, my king, that you and I alone without more help might fight this battle out to-day."

"Why, now you have unwished five thousand men," said the king laughing, "and that pleases me more than to wish us one more. God be with you all."

A.D. 1415.

So they went into battle tired as they were. The brave English let loose such a shower of arrows that, as at Creçy, the white feathers of the arrows filled the air like snow, and the French fled before them.

The Earl of Suffolk was wounded, and as he lay dying, the Duke of York, his great friend, wounded to death, dragged himself to Suffolk's side and took him by the beard and kissed his wounds, and cried aloud –

"Tarry, dear Cousin Suffolk,
My soul shall keep thine company to heaven.
Tarry, sweet soul, for mine, then fly abreast,
As in this glorious and well-foughten field
We kept together in our chivalry."

Then he turned to the king's uncle, the Duke of Exeter, and took his hand and said: "Dear my lord, commend my service to my sovereign."

Then he put his two arms round Suffolk's neck, and the two friends died together. But the battle was won.

Peace was made with France, and to seal the peace Henry married the French princess, Katherine. A little son was born to them at Windsor, and was called Henry of Windsor, Prince of Wales; he was afterwards Henry the Sixth. When Henry the Fifth knew he was going to die, he called his brothers together and gave them good advice about ruling England and France, and begged them to take great care of his little son. Henry the Sixth was not a year old when his father died, and he was crowned at once.

One of the finest English poems we have, was written about the Battle of Agincourt.

I.

Fair stood the wind for France
When we our sails advance,
Nor now to prove our chance
Longer will tarry;
But putting to the main
At Caux, the mouth of Seine,
With all his martial train,
Landed King Harry.

II.

And turning to his men,

Quoth our brave Harry then,
Though they be one to ten,
Be not amazed.
Yet have we well begun;
Battles so bravely won
Have ever to the sun
By fame been raised.

III.

And for myself (quoth he)
This my full rest shall be,
England ne'er mourn for me,
Nor more esteem me.
Victor I will remain,
Or on this earth lie slain,
Never shall she sustain
Loss to redeem me.

IV.

Poitiers and Cressy tell
When most their pride did swell,
Under our swords they fell;
No less our skill is
Then when our grandsire great,
Claiming the regal seat,
By many a warlike feat
Lopped the French lilies.

V.

They now to fight are gone,
Armour on armour shone,
Drum now to drum did groan,

To hear was wonder;
That with the cries they make,
The very earth did shake,
Trumpet to trumpet spake,
Thunder to thunder.

VI.

With Spanish yew so strong,
Arrows a cloth-yard long
That like to serpents stung,
Piercing the weather;
None from his fellow starts,
But playing manly parts,
And like true English hearts,
Stuck close together.

VII.

When down their bows they threw
And forth their bilbos drew,
And on the French they flew,
Not one was tardy;
Arms were from shoulders sent,
Scalps to the teeth were rent,
Down the French peasants went –
Our men were hardy.

VIII.

This while our noble king,
His broadsword brandishing,
Down the French host did ding,
As to o'erwhelm it.
And many a deep wound lent
His arms with blood besprent.

And many a cruel dent
Bruised his helmet.

IX.

Upon Saint Crispin' day
Fought was this noble fray.
Which fame did not delay
To England to carry.
O when shall Englishmen
With such acts fill a pen,
Or England breed again
Such a King Harry?

HENRY VI., THE BABY KING.

www.ingramcontent.com/pod-product-compliance
Lightning Source LLC
Chambersburg PA
CBHW052215240426
43670CB00037B/636